Amazon Kindle Direct Publishing©.

Blumaniterriano

Sienna V. Feruzi

This vessel--
This treasure chest;
This courtyard,
This microbe
Crawling along in a sea of stars
Exhales to feel Your exhale on her outer layer,
On her inner light;
Don't blow out the candle,
Just show the flame You Are. There.
You Are Its Air.

Chest.

Why is it you make me feel alive and dead
The summer meets the winter
So warm & lively,
But cold, instead
Why is it you make me feel unreal and old
Why is it?... You're not right for me,
But you sizzle, and fizzle my soul
And you are not the one for me
Yet give me the same warm energy
Here and here, 'most anywhere they show
All of the people love this duo,
But the Lord has said I must gooooo!

Five Twenty.

I don't think God has a gender
Maybe It has both sexes
Maybe It has a third type and maybe even a fourth
Maybe none at all,
I don't think many plan to give Him His rightful fame,
I just hope we get to see His black-brown face
Jesus isn't white.
And neither is God.
If you think He is,
You're giving in to the Fraud.
I need to truly communicate with and love myself...
I can't do it without Your Help.
I know I'm a black queen–
"He's not my color"'s self-depriving.
It's hateful, it's foolish, it's blind to the spectrum of humanity.
It's blind, it's egotistic, it's impatient to the heart you cannot see
And the heart that you can.
Our body's made all of the same matter,
His heart, something you may ne'er encounter,
Ne'er shatter.
We are not God
We are just men
                    But we can connect once again.

Once Again

I want to bite and twist your upper lip
Up to your ear;
I want to taste you down,
Chase all your fears
I need your hands on my side
And your tongue
On my pride

I love your body
I need your heat
I crave your eyes and breathing
As I stand on your feet.

You're almost all I feel I have sometimes,
No one else understands
That's why I always need you to hold my hand.
I hate school.
And you're cool.

I think I've completely become your fool.

Only one with time well spent
Is the one who is meant
To be who I run to,
May be heaven-sent.

I miss you. Every moment I'm not with you.
I need you-- every moment that I breathe.
You'll always set my heart at ease.

And be my pink evening's breeze.

Fool Ish in Pink.

I want to be an island,
Be one with an island
That can make me smile like I've seen Life and its essence itself,
Like I've never seen pure happiness and been so in the present
ever before,
Like I had seen God,
Like I had breathed and knew
what it meant,
What it meant to smell the sun sparkles and feel the dust rush by
me
As I stepped out,
Out into a dew-dimmed forest by the sea.
A sea of memories to come and memories that have been born.
Under a sky of Agape and Freedom.

Getaway.

Let me be of light
Let me hear, understand and Know Your Word,
Let me feel like I'm becoming Your close friend,
Let me be humbled and gracious and loving to others with
differences and blindness and carelessness again,
Let me feel You and Your care again,
Let me feel me again,
Let me speak up for You and for friends and family when the
times come,
Let me speak up for myself when the times come,
Let me speak up for righteousness when the times come,
Let me feel Joy again. Let me feel like me again.
Now I see the relation between one's behavioral ways and
identity...
Now I see why they say, "Be true to who you are."
It's never too late for a fresh start!

Like Me Again.

I wanna suck your candy cane till you're spasming and shaking
in pleasure.
I wanna glaze you in my saliva and icing from my sweet sugar
plum.
I want you to forget what you smell like and forget what I smell
like,
Because everything will smell like our most inner parts will cling
to every drop of the air
And mingle with every stream of sweet candle-lit aromas,
As we mingle together as one in our room of romance.
I wanna obey your every command and flavor your every meal
And brighten your every morning, if just for a weekend alone.
Alone with you. You and your strong, sleek dark and strong
figure.
Oooh, baby, you know I don't want anyone else's.
Mmm, my king, you are so delightful.

A Mid-Summer Prayer.

I want my words to live longer and maybe brighter than myself.
I want to speak words that breathe light and life,
Not only into situations, but in
To souls,
To perspectives,
To emotions
And individuals
Tiny and great,
I want to emanate God;
I want to radiate joy, grace and favor.
As they have punctured me--
I shall become a jack-o-lantern.
Lord, make me free but disciplined again!
Call it freedumb for now, 'cause I act like
I'm free but I'm not moving smartly,
And I wanna be but I'm slow enough to think
I can be so without the focused determination.

Freedumb.

Pale lavender fuschia veils this Indigo Sky.
White twinkly stars are smiling, feelin' nigh.
Exhale and the air swirls gray;
Today was a pure green day
Tickle Me Pink moments of wisdom,
Sunshine Yellow dreams spoken
Sienna questions, worries
Light against a blood red determination,
Striped by Navy hopes,
Today was a pure green day--
Productive but hard...
Ponderous but encouraged
Tired as gray.
Optimistic as lime!
Scarletly divine.
Excited as magenta
Unimpressed as eggshell.
Mannn, I'm gonna give 'em hell.

Preparation Phase.

Make Love to me for who You really are,
Whoever that is,
And for who I really am.
Be intimate with me, oh God,
I'm calling for I'm but a lamb
My shepherd is the only One who knows the ways around the
mountains, gorges, canyons and streams, I need to return back to
me and they say I need to return back into You,
Barely feel it anymore
But simultaneously do,
I desperately, ultimately, emphatically
Need You.

Astray.

I believe you can fly
You messed up the whole FBI
All you wanted was some girls that's teens
A cold beer 'n' chicken wings
I believe you can soar
Waiting on the court decision was no bore
I believe
You can sail
I believe that you'll go to jail
Stay for life now boy you'll grow stale---
See you running thru those Guadalajara cells---
You will live behind bars
No more running, rocking with the stars---
I believe you can fly
Yeah your tale was a lie---
There in jail you will die---
Unless you turn your life round now to Jeez
He's already given you His keys---
If you can change this
Maybe He'll rearrange this
But I still think you a perv-
I ain't gotta get your word
Boy, from you, I would swerve
You ain't gotta take my word!---
I believe you can fly--*

Fly.

*R. Kelly. *R*. Jive Records, 1996.

Won't spend no 10 seconds
On somethin' less than a dime!
Won't give up all my dignity on y'all
Cause I got my own life
I got my own precious time
Ain't givin' it all up to the boss
'Less I want my hopes to get lost--
Will I retire on time,
Will I have to wait for my rounds 'round the table each year?
Will my every bi-week
Cause me to binge on the edge of fear?-
In a coin toss!

Toss.

I am your milk
you are my honey
You of European flour
and I, of Omega cocoa,
I am your milk
you are my honey
We combined
Make Greek Yogurt
in a place above the clouds
Make our dreams come out loud
into our nostrils
Sprinkled in our mouths
You are a dream: alive.
A dream: a life.

Three Ten.

This little daughter can't do it on her own
She can't think with little strength
Too much on her mind
With little exercise
Stress kills motivation
Too much sleep deprivation
But she gave her life
So she might live
And she's realized

The power Your light gives
So her dependence is dropped
At your Holy feet
She knows the blessings, the fate she'll meet
You've already paved golden her life street
She maintains her stride
She fumbles still
But keeps her head high
Awed by Your will
Your freedom and Your desire
For her, a mild, lowly child
She always shall admire and stay amazed
At the boundless, brightest grace
Most brilliance
Never in chances of millions
Would she get a love like this elsewhere

So she can't change course
She will succeed--
Now she's off her high horse.
Self-dependence is a mild disease of faith--
It doesn't kill it, but brushes it slightly away...

Cinco Cinco.

I have a situmuhwation
I have a friend who seems forsaken
Who doesn't seem to know God
And seldom seems to care
Who sometimes searches and listens
But doesn't see how unaware
And how deprived they've been
And how alive and free they could be
If they allowed Him to give them victory
If only they read the Word, just a lil' more
If only they prayed and prayed and prayed
To see what He has in store
And didn't think that God would condemn and deplore;

Prayer is never dangerous
And through it, God NEVER condemns!
If only they accepted Jesus' heart so He could fully revive them.

Maybe all I should do now is pray for him.

Cinco Five.

God, I need you to give me a booster,
So I can holla like a rooster
And strut out my nest
Wit dis oomph in my chest
'Cause I know dat I'm blessed
And can take on the rest
O' life!

Some Rappers Are Evil. But My God Is Good!!

I yearn to lead you to a place unseen
A Wonder Land divine
Like a dream
Another experience
So serene.
No chaos, in or out,
No hooligans or "fooled again"s runnin' about
No insecurities, grudges, aches or doubt
Just something new and never known
Something beyond the Mind: blown.
Something money can never buy
And somewhere for lovers, no matter how shy;
A place where lovers are always free:
I want to give you Eternity.

I want to give you the world and so much more,
But you don't understand what's in store.
For you don't know how God loves you.
And you don't know what my God can do.
My God will never judge or abandon,
But somehow, He's misunderstood and taken for granted....
I only wish that you'd be willing
To see that my God's so thrilling
I only wish He'd help open those eyes,
For I can only imagine how you'd be soooo surprised
God doesn't just change-- he heals and magnifies lives!

My God can remove the Darkness that is bothering you
And He wants to be Your God, too...
He can prove how much stronger and Greater is He,
If only,
If Only--
You could see.
This yearning's my love,
But it stems from Him,
It's all for you,
This Wonder Land's

Not just in another world,
It becomes real today in many, in adults, boys and girls.
It becomes real to all,
As long as they pray and answer His call.
He wants salvation not just for a select few–
Sadly not all accept it,
But I'm begging you.
I need to take you
To a place unseen...
A Wonder Land divine
Like a dream––
Nothing about it's grim.
This yearning's
Not about my love and me
If only,
If Only––
You would see.

Then you could have my jubilee.

This burning urge is supernatural, I can't explain––
I just want to ease up your pain
And so does God––
He always has...
He's done it for me,
Life won't be easy,
But overall, He'll set you free:
If only,
If Only––
You would see!

If Only.

Why always keep our eyes on the prize
Like money's all that matters in our lives?!
If that's where our treasure lies
Our hearts will be buried in the quicksands of deceit,
The muds of a life that this world cheats
From which it is so hard to retreat
But it is quite rewarding
To let it go

Release our minds in forward tow
Our hearts cold as snow
Souls as numb as oceans, no wind to blow
We need to see, we should fulfill our needs
And those are to have a life that's about so much more than greed
A world from which the wealthy and humble feed
Truce isn't always bestowed

Yet Boaz redeems and nurtures Ruth
With no expectations or harsh demands
On her little heart and hands
For she bent low and planted seeds
That she and all the great world needs
In her heart and those of others
'Cause we're all Sisters and Brothers...
A seed that will your heart and spirit enhance,
That will provide for you a second chance,
And live out to our truest, boldest dance
To give humility, empathy some more romance
We need to help the Kingdom advance
So, we should give our all to God,
Ensuring evil will not over-trod
Our perspectives, our sight,
He gave free will with All His Might,
If we just let Him plant some seeds
Within us and still believe,

We can bring our friends to a brighter eternity
And a brighter life right here
Where to others, and ourselves, we are sincere
And kind, and free, and out of fear

Since we learn to live our greatest, brightest, boldest dance,
Because God gave us one more chance.
So we should give our all to God
And evil will not over-trod!

Treasure Dance.

Thought that I couldn't breathe and eat and walk and roam and
sleep with no You,
Couldn't plan and endure and grow old with just me and Who
‐‐ ‐‐
But I'm pretty much survivin' okay
I think I'm gonna be alright‐‐
Doubted 'bout much more dismay,
But I really missed your presence last night.

You attended to my every need,
Made me feel like I was inside a dream,
Oh, how I've missed all the care you made!
I knew I couldn't get all the memories to fade!
I miss you enthralling my neck
I miss engulfing your hair
I miss holding you, soothing you everywhere.
For now I've found what makes me happiest
Is when my lover feels the best,
More than however I felt or feel.
I want you to know my love was real,

But I ain't half as sad as I thought I'd be
Since my main Obsession's become me‐‐
And not just in a selfish way, though,
Gotta take care of myself, you know‐‐
I was just doing what I wanted
And not listening to the Lord instead
I did what Sienna thought felt right for her,
Though what glittered wasn't gold
Or even worth a tiny chunk of old...
Silver.

So, I guess my point is
I'm getting over you

I know you sensed a lil emptiness too
And you know we'll always be the best of friends
Whose story will never, ever end!

26

Friends.

This woman is traveling
Humming in her head and heart
For a love to boost this surreal new start
I'm not really searching but I'm missing
I'm missing something but I don't feel a hole or much *doubt*
I find no reason to give a pout
For I know what the Lord is all about
I know He's gonna work it out
He'll find you
He'll bring you to me
I don't need to care for now
Just lean on and see

I gotta take a rest,
Alone time with the Lord,
I gotta read, invest,
Sketch my memories in the Sword.
So, I'll be ready for love and war
And feel our diligence has let us soar
No need to fret,
Already won the bet--
I'm counting on the Lord

Six One.

Take a hike
There's a tornado in my stomach
A hurricane in my head
I gotta go out runnin'
I gotta breathe rich and clear instead;
I cant stand bein' scrunched up
Much longer, too much stress
Or tasks and to-dos keepin me a mess
Along with all they left me with
I gotta clear my head
I gotta feel my heart
A lil' better, physically,

But not just in that way, of course,
No not just that, indeed.
I gotta prove myself I'm strong but not just that cliche
I gotta make sure I know myself and care for myself each day
Or else I'll become
Nothing but them
And to be a bum
Is the worst for sure
Bein' grouchy always
And barely can endure...

Maybe run a marathon
Before this super quick years gone
Maybe learn to ride my bike
Farther than I've ever been
Maybe go for a hike
I'm right by this mountain
Maybe try 'n' give a motorcycle a different kind of spin
Maybe try a new type of dance
Oi, decisions; where to begin?
But that's just the start
I need to test a new type of Art!

Need.

29

I'm a wordsmith of justice,
A witch or a joker
I am an announcer. I'm a fighter
It's in my blood-- always has been
You will be here today,
Gone tomorrow, I'm cold, warm, blame my sorrow...

What I Am.

I weaken the urge
I'm killin the surge
The need, the glue, the strong yearning
That I know is vision-burning
And not worth the share
'Cause we can't end up in the lair
Of harm and selfish selflessness without a
    care

But I still want you, feel you everywhere
And know I'm mainly feeling myself
But I can't be with no one else
For now I feel it's hard to live
Without reaching as close as I can
To you, to show you how I am
And how much I enjoy talking, just us 2
Although we know we can't guess when
    the next time I'll see you..

Six Fourteen.

I tried to come up with a couple ways I could complain,
But all that I could really quite explain
Is how much peace I've gained.
I don't know how much but I'm pretty content
I think a lot of this time is gettin' well spent
I ought to relax more
We all really should
Some rejuvenation could be what I need,
But not just from gettin' a little more sleep
....

Five Twenty-Seven.

I'm paralyzed,
You're in the front of my eyes
And you won't. go. away.,
You were my light,
You were the shadow in my shade,
The breeze on my hottest days,
The pink and gold of a sunrise haze,
You were the ground under my feet,
You were the smile folks loved to greet,
I feel you now when I see injustice,
I feel you when I see true love,
I know you are the voice of my happiness and patience;

You'll always be my baptismal dove
And the one who encouraged me to stay confident and kind
Who taught me to never be left behind
For I am special, just how I am.
I'll always have that Avery glam.

I'm paralyzed but I'm motivated
Because of you I've become elated
To have this life I have to live,
If only with you, for you I could give

Another walk along the bridge
Or through the park
Or at the store
I'll always, always want some more.

But I'll have the time, I'll get the chance,
Once I meet you again.
I love you.

Dear Mema,

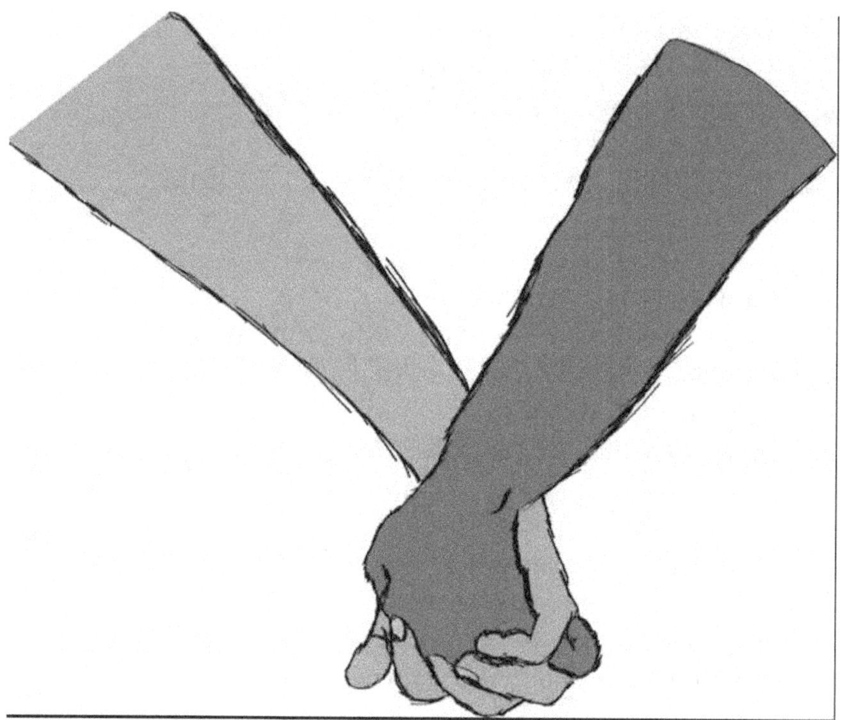

Arrogance is the fuel of Ignorance, the 16-Wheeler which runs
over any car, pedestrian or squirrel of Wisdom.
Arrogance is an enemy of common sense
Arrogance always hinders repentance,
Arrogance eliminates the chance of you not giving your stupid,
useless five cents.
That is enough,
I will not stall.
That is enough,
If you want to fall.
That is enough,
And that is all.

Seven Ten.

Mi abuela murió.
I see a l'ange in every other woman here today.
And every other day.
I feel like I'm in the outer rim of the eye of a tornado
This place is crazy,
Too much to take in
Too much, no doubt
Not enough taken in fully
Not enough to breathe out
Not enough to explain
Not enough to work or debate about
Only enough to self-consult with and cry out to God for;

Inward I look and listen for His voice or a reminder from His
Word:
What have I known, what have I heard?
Just a little cheeriness in the environment
And I'm revitalized and feeling Heaven-sent
Now I feel more like I can do it all again.

Just 10 more hours and I can filter it all in.
This day was busy,
I don't want to rewind,
But now I understand more how some things seem so hard to find,
A little bit of patience, a lot a bit of charm, a little bit of
gratefulness
Will never do you harm,
The Lord giveth, and the Lord taketh away--
What have you thanked and asked God for today?

Seven Eleven.

When a white man sees a young black woman and assumes she's
just a crazy girl with no big career plan,
That's called a wrongful assumption.
When a man decides a woman's hair color, curliness or length
and sex is too unprofessional for a salary equal to her male
contemporary,
That's called sharing without caring.
When an Asian woman glares at any teenage black boy or girl
for no apparent reason and without any interaction for probable
cause,
That's called, "sly indecency."

When a white man doesn't wanna visit a friend's friendly, warm
and welcoming Christian black church more than once or twice,
or not at all, even though his black friend and many black people
can happily visit or join a white friendly, warm and welcoming
church because they're married to a white person or feel
comfortable around friendly, warm and welcoming white
Christians, just because he isn't used to being the minority for one,
or two, or three parts of one, or two, or three days in his life while
his black friends or comrades or acquaintances at least,

if he has any, or strangers, are quite used to being minorities three
hundred and sixty-five days a year, every year of their lives,
three-hundred sixty-six on leap years,

That's called, "staying in one's shell" or "hypocrisy" or "out with
the old, and in with the... old."

When that male customer at my restaurant's staring me up and
down with that look on his face,
That shit's called micro-rape.
When a white woman assumes a black guy in the same room or
in a store is a dire threat to the safety of all,

That's called ringing the wrong alarm.

I think these pretty much are called "f***-you"s to others who
grandly encompass the remainder of the subparts of society.
I think these are called "unfair things adults do, even though they
generally explain to their kids not to do so."
I think even though white men make up the cause of literally over
99% of public massacres, we are more afraid of other men for
stupid reasons that have been shoved into our minds every day.

I think that even though women of any and all races can be
"slutty" and rough and "cray'", some groups are picked out and
called out the most for the stupidest reasons.

And we've swallowed, digested and pooped out these lies into our
daily lives.
Can we smile at each other a little more, please?
Can we not assume that we own women's bodies, even with our
eyes?

Can we not be so quick to glare and hunt down an imaginary
enemy? The enemy is your mind. Okay?

Can We.

You got sand in your eyes?
You got sand or something?
You don't own me.
If anything, you owe me.
I'm done.
I'm not about done.
I'm done.
Kill your misogyny.
In the name of Jesus.

Starin' at Me Like I Owe You Somethin'.

My lifes a mess
All i can says God bless
I am that child
Gonna have my own*
Cuz I got too much
To not light up that Throne
gotta keep my familys whole minds blown
Doin things id never known
I could, be more than the woman
That i "should"
Cuz i god'a B the woman i was made to be
No matter what my past--
Or peer-- or maven-made plans foresee

Four Twenty-Two.

*Billie Holiday. *Solitude*. Edward B. Marks Music, 1941.

I've walked and run a lot more than you ever will in at least half
of your life.
I keep seeing, I keep feeling the honeysuckle chamomile sweet
atmosphere,
Or the memories renewed, the deja vu,
And I know how the paths lay ahead for me
And spread for me,
Less dread for me.
I am stronger,
I got more cardio,
I make my own wind,
With the wind, you go,
What have you seen and experienced?
Have you even given my streets and corners a glance?
I whip through the air and the sun knows me,
I fly 'round a turn and bring a hill to its knees;
I stroll past a garden, I storm with the breeze,
These paths, they love me,
They give me such ease,
Since they've kissed my mind with many years of glad-mad
memories.

I Know.

I don't hate the fog,
The fog reminds me my world isn't mine
Nature is on so many levels and sometimes it has to stoop down
low--
That doesn't mean it only works for me, though.
The fog reminds me there are invisible tiny things in life that often
are the most essential,
And when the world gets cold,
They may need to cling together
To block out and blind the predator
And veil the prey, the multitudes, with a serene divine cloud.
Like an anointing on a young enchanted child
Who's tired of thinking,
Wants to finally think out loud.

Fog and Tininess.

This small lady is mad
She is disgusted.
She is glad
When they get busted.
But right now, she's feelin'
Low 'n' weak,
She doesn't know what to think,
She's just gettin' started, she's on the brink...
She's considered naming her first child Patience,
Not for the little boy or girl,
But for herself to regain the memories, at times when--
Sometimes you can breathe in and out and in and out
Again,
But ya have to wait a lil' longer for a response to each question.

Me, Now.

Something, someone keeps telling me to give you a call,
But what good would it do at all?
You don't even stalk
On me,
So what am I doing?
You don't belong with me anymore
Now I have got to see what He has in store.
My future feels torn,
Just a little,
I want you by my side
But I also want to hide.
I know what I want,
But I don't think it's in you.
So why do I keep acting lost, bitter, confused?

Nine Ten.

They say, *Go Into Your Quiet Corner,*
But where is a corner without chanting walls and tempting windows,
Without a yelling voice and cackling laughter?
Where, oh where is a silence--
A stillness of air, a coma of sound--
No buzzing, no music, no humming, no chatter;
Maybe a sweet smooth soft tune, no, this matters;
I need to see my mind but not hear so much from me,
Take some breaths, know He'll end the fear in me...

Where to Go.

'Heart' doesn't rhyme with 'hard'
And 'heart' doesn't rhyme with 'soft'
'Heart' just rhymes with 'art'
That's why I'm in my loft
We can't play telephone
If your word is your heart
And your heart can't recall
It's first beating
Before the fall.
You can't send a letter
In a mailbox full of cobwebs, scratches and shadows
If you wish for your friend to open it up.

Wishes.

Didn't judge the innocent, breath-taking ___.
Didn't wish harm or a selfish wish on the sweetest, treasured,
loving ___.
Sashayed fingertips o'er the hands of the eager, mesmerized ___.
Read the wrinkles of the layers, of the lips, of the bowels, of the
thighs of the poised, enchanted ___.
Smelled the needs and cares and joys of the rich, yet modest ___.
Communed with the lightest and deepest wisps of delight of the
glad, satisfied ___.

But that wasn't enough.
She lost her satisfaction as the hourglass flipped, the snow globe
tipped over--
And the wants of a nasty devil fell down low as the wants of the
Holy Ghost emerged
And she found her dignity and the remainder of her identity in
Christ.
Everything he did had been right, but everything he did had been
empty of The Truest Love,
And so his actions were
    Void.
and
          Useless.

Since his identity was in his works 'n' attempts, but
Not in God's Finest Hopes 'n' Dreams,

And his name became Empty Wishes
And hers became Christ-like Flight
And she danced alone, without him,
With all. her. might.
*You had all these names for me but not a name for yourself. And
def'n'tey not a sacred one.*

Twelve Twenty-One.

Oh, I tried to protect you,
I shouted and pounded and kicked to do for you,
But I am not you and you are not me,
And you are not my baby,
So I had to pray and set you free...

Oh, I pray someday you'll belong to God
    And then belong to me,
Self-Harmed.

Twelve Twenty-Two.

I hate my mind.
I hate my spirit.
I hate it all, sometimes.

But then, I pause, relax my jaws,
and see: the mistake's not bigger than me;

We hit our heads
We hit our feet
We hit our groins against the wall sometimes.
Can't make reason/rhyme
To it,
All-star,
Then we gaze up, pull our boots up,
And hold hands as we walk
To speak: we will not settle but we will have our dry seasons,
& That's OK.

They grind their teeth,
Release their sheaths,
They wanna rage war, many times.
But soon, surrender,
They see we're sinners--
And we can't always express angst and greed
Without paying heed:
To the knowing, we are one wave, one blade, one speck, one rave,
one stage, one star, one time, one heart;
One blood.
Least we can share's a real, real love.

I, & They...

If I could write you, world,
If I could write you what is up here
In my lil' head,
I think you could do the same,
Just read a lot first, instead,
You read a lot, you see the patterns, the images, the feels, irony,
You see how the sound- and aesthetic- matching work in
harmony,

You make it do you,
So you won't be me or another,
You make the piece of paper your phone for your sister or brother,
You make it really familial and personal and clear,
Or murky and unattached for whoever that day, month or year

You do whatever you want to do,
You make it your imaginary land,
A place you can run off to
And send others, hand in hand
And leave it etched in the memories of their brains,
Like your own signature on their own sand,
'Cause anything can spark up
When you've read good and have pen in hand

Was, was that a lucid poem?
Is, is this some lucid dream?
Is this all a lucid dream?
Is this ALL a lucid dream?!?!?

Twelve Twelve.

I can't call you "Daddy"
And you can't call me "baby doll"
When you treated me like Raggedy Annie
And my dad was not my nanny,
No that's not cute or casual or sexy
I ain't never gon' be nobody's Becky;
And why the fuck would you used to say,
"Girls can say no but that doesn't mean you stop!"
And laugh with the boys like you'd reached the mountaintop
Was popularity and good times all that would echo into your
next decade
Or was that all a false truth and hope
You told, and retold, and retold yourself
Till it showed up as a facade?
And yes, I know how to pronounce "facade"
And yes, I know you'd hit pubescent youth,
But didn't it ring in your ears ever since,
Didn't you know that'd be the truth?
And now you have used it to do dirty deeds,
But at least it kept feeding your undying greed,
At least it left me to just bleed, bleed, bleed.

Three Six.

I was the reason to your rhyme;
I was the water to your flour
I was the player to your punk
I couldn't take all of your power;
You were the rake to my grass
You were the king to my empire
You were the kisser of my ass
You could never be another liar
We were like baby blue and bright pink,
We made a glorious violet with no ink,
Could do just that and not even think,
Everywhere we went, we lit up and danced
In the light of violet,
But now that violet's become violent
And I can't remain
You never left a stain,
But I'm not the same and I'm lonely and sick
If I stay, so,
Goodbye,
First Love.

Bye.

Blumaniterrian,
working for a Blue-Green World as humanity's librarian--
I did a good job working it.
it birthed me,
no cesarean
we were here to cultivate
not brand, but make
whether full-on agrarian
or urban as them in their turbans
no matter how colorful or gray
we have history to create
we have new winds to breathe
new boats to rock
no looking back, just check the clock!
you see, the trees,
the seas,
they're crying,
its urgency
as clear as the sameness, and difference, and plainness of you and
me!
here is my home.
I can live here 'most forever:
past the dreams of all great centenarians,
working for a Blue-Green World as humanity's librarian!

Two Twenty-Two/Blumaniterrian.

I'm a shy 'n' bubbly 'n' sarcastic Spelman woman
And I'm 'bout to bring my champ fam on in
I got my cousins from Howard
Here to bash on all y'all cowards
Albany States's been comin through
You see my face so y'know I got my crew--
I got Clark's great band
They gon' tear it down
I got my Morehouse man
You know th's ain't no foolin' 'round,
You know FAMU,
It parades on for us too
Been runnin' with A&T
You know they all got me!

Band.

All my friends
Have hundreds of pics
from their childhood,
Mine are good,
But few.
Open box of trinkets--
Long- loved possessions,
Would just come to think it,
You'd learn a lesson
from one quick view.

Achievement,
Quickstar
"Always putting others first",
"Can you find the...",
I'll always remember
access code,
@Yahoo.com
It's Your Birth,
hate from you and your,
Media center
LM-TF,
I'm like a really funny, nice,
Made in China,
October November,
Hopefully,
        your friend,
            Liz,
Ecuador
Please call if you are coming,
Summer in our backyard,
Run Faster,
Run Farther,
Stationery,
139201

Smiles

Each one of them takes me back
To the flash of a picture
Days that have been turned and almost,
But not quite, been forgotten
The ages of a scrapbook in the back of
My mind

Not exactly a treasure
Not at all a mystery
Something I hold on to
The only thing I can hold on to
When I am bored
Or excited to enjoy myself,
Have peace with
Myself and my past.

View.

I don't want a man squeezing some of me tight
Like I need it to set me loose
I don't need no one goin' for me like I'm a papaya dripping with
juice
I ain't no fruit or the essential aroma essence of
        it
I don't want no one sniffin'
It like a villain, it's just mine and it's the Lord's,
        and it's that for a reason
I've let go of burning summers
It's a selfish spring
I'm in my due season,
Don't need anyone
Expanding my waters
Drying my skins
Preparing for slaughter
In places we'll never venture again
I don't want no more pajama saunas !
I'm done with lust; I'm done with love!!
I don't want to see **no son's** eyes or thighs
From below or from above
I don't want to hear a man's deep sighs and
        mutters...
I don't want him gazing, caressing, another of my udders,
I don't want my nipples to be nuzzled
Nor do I want another man to cuddle,
I left it back up on a shelf--
I didn't leave nothin' muddled.
I don't want to be a goddess or angel for no one
        else
Always hours later, days later, nights later,
Crawling into corners,
Away from myself!
I don't want to be a solace spot,
A satisfaction siren, safety zone,
Sensual snack.
I want ALL my restitution, independence,

I want ALL my dignity back!

One Three.

You gave me barely a fourth of your own
When I'd given you almost my whole heart
I was almost completely open about my earlier years,
Until you introduced a fear
Because you never were so clear,
You coward.
So, we never really made it
And you shunned and stoned me
So the memory's never faded
You left no piece,
No pieces worthy or fruitful,
And no peace,
Under your crying, smiling eyes, too youthful,
So I hate you, let you go,
Yet I'm reminded each time life snows.

Snowy Sunlight.

I let a part of me die for you
And a new one sprouted bright for us two
I let another start to crumble and fade
But this one was too strong for me, babe,
You opened up all of your heart,
I opened up all of mine
But yours wasn't half as good,
You shook me up,
I felt misunderstood;
I had to find what was the fix--
Kept denying what escaped the Crucifix,
Had to get to the water, the desert's parched me dry,
Had to deny us and lust,
Had to finally die
And in my place there blossomed a pearl grander than a great
merchant's best,
I'm glad I talked with Jesus
And got that bull---- off my chest!
....

I remember, I remember it all, but
The besos, the besos didn't have the same effect, the same patterns,
colors, the same wavelengths, the same pull.
And your inhales in my exhales didn't smell the same, feel the
same--
All I cared about were God's exhales on my brain...
He was whispering, sometimes telling, sometimes shouting, at least
I was shouting, ringing in my ear,
In my ear, in my ear,... in my inner ear...
And His breath tasted sweeter, tingled of wisdom and rebuke and
love at its truest, purest form;
I could not deny The Lord.

Twelve Twenty-Eight.

What do u when nothing by nothing seems to stick?
When everybody, every member wants to lay it thick?
When all your hair falls,
Your soul calls
For you to pick
You scratch and scrape
Too afraid to cut away
You like the rush, the hurry and the toughened pain;
You can't get out
You've always had to be a part
Of something lame
That will not change
Even with a brand new start

What & When.

What is love?
Where is love?
When is love?
...

When's my time?
Time for these chapters? Those episodes?
When's my end time?
Why's she staring at me? Why's he glaring at me? Why's He
smiling on me?
I don't get it.
I never will.
With time, I'll get it,
   Though.

*I Was Conceived Only Less Than Tres Decades Back and yet, I
Sometimes Feel Old, I Sometimes Feel Wise, I'm Sometimes
Confused.*

My God ain't fake
My judgment ain't mistakes
Unless I don't follow His ways
I strive to make tomorrow a greater day--
A greater walk, a loving talk, a wiser stroll
I have to adhere to His every scroll
There's nothing greater than taking His hand
He's already given a glimpse of the promised land!
When you learn to fall for Christ,
It's never, ever blinding--
When you give your all to Christ,
It's sight and hope you're finding;
He reveals so much when you allow Him to keep in touch
He holds back His wrath when you let Him plan and do the math
There's nothing weak about making Him your rod and your
strength--
Without Him, we can only make it through for a short length!
There's only satisfaction
When you obey and love The Craftsman.
You don't have to first "fix up" your life--
Without Him, you can't even do that perfect 'n' right!
You gotta just let Him save
And give up claiming you're the brave!
Mm, isn't He so good?
Isn't He so, so good, for all?!
Take up on Him, take Him,
Lest you fall!
He gives us the option
So there is no force...
It's up to you to follow His course!
Cuz it's demons that you'll be binding
And it's never, ever blinding-
It's sight and hope you're finding!

Finding.

God, now I guess I'll just say, You can have Your way
Use all of my clay
To mold me and restore me
So I know more for Your glory...
God, I don't know how to wait
On this promise
I can't hesitate
So it's hard to sit and listen but thanks to You, it's easier to hear:
I and My Voice will be with you throughout the year!

The Year.

Young me didn't know what they would mean
When they said not everything was as it seemed
Now I've sensed the shadows,
I've heard from the light,
I've held the truth on my tongue's tip
Told their lies without death wish;
I Am Strong.
I covered for adults
Even though I felt a piece of me was smothered in their un-love,
They felt comfort in living for a lie
They didn't want my truth to make their atmosphere die,
They kicked part of my identity, outing the cold, never-ending
rain,
And I thought, and I hoped I would never feel it again...
So as a kid
I grew up through all that shit,
And as an adult
I did the same for someone who was like a child
Put all my respect on him
Though he made me defiled
And so that drenched cold part of me just went into a coma--
Numb, done, it was exiled.
I thought my energy was depleted,
       But now I'm speaking out and without a doubt,
       I haven't been defeated.
I know how to strengthen and reawaken that special part of me,
With numbers and the remainder of My Voice,
              I'll set other Girls Free!

Twelve Twenty-Seven.

I love seeing your smile from 100 feet away. I love feeling your warm arms around me, your smooth cuddly chest under me when I first see you again after a long while. You know how to make me smile and feel like a queen better than anyone I've ever met. I love holding you until you swoon and can't help but bend down closer to my face so our mouths can join and tell each other, "Oh, there you are again, of course. How I've missed you," without speaking till our hearts start pounding so hard in the streets till our bodies can sense the louder vibrations pulling us in closer to each other until we decide to stroll side by side, hand meshed into hand, as one. That's why I love your smile. More than just the cute dimples. I read you well. And you read me too.

Even when we're far apart.

Twelve Twenty-8.

I gasp in the nature of Nayyirah, I gaze o'er the rawness of Rupi,
I get gladdened by the diction of Emily– oh, I am saddened by the
mood of Maya;
I heard a girl say her dad hurt her in the coochie,
And I spiral into fear, cuz I know she's not the only one kinda,
Kinda sorta feelin' stabbed and ignored
And burned and explored
Oh, where is the Lord?

Is it a man's world
When women run it all, in front of and behind the curtains,
below the surface,
Really?

Does anyone else around this holy space know what I'm feeling?
We are drowning in misery and blame
And I don't know who to trust to pull me up
And no one's noticing the horror when they look me in the face,
Cuz my head's above water,
So it seems.
My head's above ice and under some other cold sheets, and the ice
is so clear to you,
You barely stare,
Cuz you think my head's above water;
I've got oxygen
And a smile so you think
I need nothing to drink
And I can breathe,
But I can't.

Three Five.

If we even breathe in a few times to speak,
Who will listen?
With the ice over our faces we glisten
And look like we're basking in light,
But each day is really a fight.

Really.

She comes in and she's completely prepared,
But each time, the guys just stare, stare, staaaarrre:
She's no mess
She won't confess
She did no wrong
What is this throng
She's a red light beam in the dark
A dot of black in Baby Pink Park
She doesn't smile
She couldn't care
She just wants to make it, make it, there;
There's gossip, befuddlement in the air

But she doesn't smile
She couldn't care
She ain't got time to stop and stare
She's got to keep focused
This chance is the fullest
To pass this test and be the best
That's all she sees
Her vision's bright,
Though the present's bleak
She could care less
What you all think
She hurts, but she must keep writing
She flinches at times, but must keep fighting.
This is just the midst, the midst of a beginning

She doesn't realize she's already winning!
They're already winning, because of her
Without this woman, they couldn't get so far,
But now they are reaching
Soon, they'll fly with comets,
Shoot with stars!
Everybody calls it progress,

This goal that they share,
They try to digress--
But she cannot care.
She must complete what has been set in stone,
A rough draft, another one, and one again,
She's getting closer, this teammate's heaven-sent!
And now they're approaching, getting pretty far,
Soon, they'll fly with comets,
Shoot with stars!
Maybe soon we'll go to Mars.

Winning, Girl

(Inspired by the film "Hidden Figures")

When I ignore the static and harsh soft sounds and all your
breath or the breath you lack,
I take a second to just, sit-- sit back!
And think of where I am and where you are
And think of how I wish to go so far
With or without some friends,
With or without certain words,
With or without certain breaths, refreshments, pauses:
You almost always get what you give.
And I want to give much,
And not just to get.
I want to change the suffering world;
I want to help, to keep it lit.
Where's your inspiration?
Where's the brightness in your eyes?
You can't let go of that light.
Your eyes, they used to be more alive.
What is your journey,
And who's on your side?
What's your destination,
Where do you make your pride?

Unspoken.

Why did I love his hair?
Because it squeaked and crinkled a new breath into me,
When I'd hold it,
Every strong, wiry spiral of its thick kinkiness would cuddle my
fingers,
Each steel loop coursing through the soft, shallow sweaty rivers of
my palms like it was a part of me
When it was a part of him
Because it came from his head and was connected to his mind and
his body
Because it laughed and lept when I'd
Embrace him,
Sharing the joy I gained when I was in his presence
Because it was a canopy over my face
When I'd swoon from his pressing gaze.
Because it shaped his smooth face
And intertwined with his ragged short beard
And I liked it.
Because Gelic made me feel like a princess of the most influential
dynasty
But feel down to Earth because– I was me–
And he was him,
And we were we...

Gelic made me feel on fire but
Feel warm and cool shamelessly, nonchalantly, boldly,
And simultaneously.
Maybe I do this just to look back upon it.
People hang to, cling to memories to have a reminiscent 'fuzzy
feel';
I don't do that.
Maybe I write this 'cause I still crush on the light, the atmosphere
of glee and glamor and affection we made,
But not on him.
I don't crush on him.
Ha–HA!

I worshipped Gelic.
Only Gelic knew how to sound intelligent as a genius
And as jokingly foolish as a Joker.
Only Gelic knew how to make me hurt down to the core
Only Gelic knew how to lighten and spring me up down to the
core
Only Gelic knew how to make me laugh
And make me stop and consider
Only Gelic knew how to piss me off till I yelled and stormed
Only to give into smiling, shrugging his childishness off.

I did not like him for his phenomenal wit or his unique intelligent
points of view.
I liked him because it all stemmed
From his light of sweetness.
 A sweetness that created a humility,
A genuine care.
And that made me
admire him so.
And made him more lively and fun and generous and made him
Admire me, too.

Gelic was a wondrous man.
But he didn't know.
He didn't care for himself unconditionally.
Mostly.
He was too hard on himself.
Mostly.
But he didn't know God, that's the rest of it.
He didn't know God.

Like, Admire, But.

you callin' me an animal
sayin' a black God's mystical
when really, He's quite biblical
I don't understand
how the ideology stays in command
we fall on our knees to pray
to a Spirit we all see as white everyday
the folks overseas who paint Him brown
would gape- we never give up our crowns
to Kum ba Yah with all, lifting loyalty
to the One Who's most Holy and of Royalty
such a shame
to put a Messiah's flesh to blame
if you're not sure
if he's real
i'll tell you a white savior
is a history steal
i'll tell you I know He lives
and to each colored sunrise, He shines
and to each colored sea, abode and heart,
He gives
out to every colored soul, every newborn,
every colorful new space, colorless snowstorm,
every creature, every flower
every weekend, every night-time, every hour.
each star-brazen Hand never makes mistakes,
now, what other [in]vulnerable history will you take
and [in]feasible stories shall you make?

Twelve Thirty-One.
holy spirit: I need more of you
rise up fill up this room
set my heart
my life
on fire
commune to salute and praise with thee

more of you
less of me
save the world
take my life
take my hand
i'll be your wife
set me free
to follow thee
more of thee
less of me
we need increase
set us free
or are we free
already
are we free already

Already.

Just 'cause my hips blends in with my waist, blends in with my
legs don't make me blend in with this space–time
You know I stand out.
Just 'cause my body's different don't mean it's got to shout.
Don't make it any louder than hers or yours,
You just want to hear it louder:
'Cause you're unexposed,
You gaze on after;
But I'm never chose,
You and your people go on with laughter
But still try to guess what's under and between all these clothes.

Four Thirty.

Thought that I couldn't breathe and eat and walk and roam and
sleep with no You,
Couldn't plan and endure and grow old with just me and
Who...-
But I'm pretty much survivin' okay
I think I'm gonna be alright-
Doubted 'bout much increased dismay;
But I really missed your presence last night.
You attended to my every need;
Made me feel like I was inside a dream,

Oh, how I've missed all the care you made!
I knew I couldn't get all the memories to fade!
I miss you enthralling my neck
I miss engulfing your hair
I miss holding you, soothing you everywhere.
For now I've found what makes me happiest
Is when my lover feels the best
More than however I felt or feel
I want you to know my love was real

But I ain't half as sad as I thought I'd be
Since my main Obsession's become me
And not just in a selfish way, though,
Gotta take care of myself, you know
I was just doing what I wanted
And not listening to the Lord instead
I did what Averi thought felt right for her
Though what glitterred wasn't gold
Or even worth a tiny chunk of old
Silver...
So, I guess my point is,
I'm getting over you,
And I know you sensed a lil dissension too
And you know we'll always be the best of friends

Whose story will never, ever end!

Story.

And neither does my face
And this body never ends, though it's infinite space.
Just 'cause my shell is an infinity shape,
Doesn't mean you have to endlessly gaze,
Just 'cause my nose is softer, more delicate and round
Than any of your kind of wife or girl you've found,
Doesn't mean I'm an ape
Just 'cause the ceiling wants to creep and hover higher
And the floor echoes too soft, too profoundly of my vibes
Doesn't mean it can't contain you either.
I go on Forever.
And so do you.
So why must my booty
Have your eyes stuck like glue?
Is that my fault,
I exist,
Do you have a clue?

We're all
In this hall
In a macro-space,
And this is what they call
A

Micro-Rape.

i feel kinda empty
but it doesn't even matter
i feel very numb and exhausted but
that's never an excuse.
where do I fit in?
I feel like we're so different,
me and The Very Few
And The Other Very Few, I guess together we make a good team
We cast a brighter light on this whole scene.

Ten Thirteen.

If you don't got a boy
You don't got no drama
If you got a man
You become a mama
But what if you just want a dude
But you don't want another role as Mom
Cuz you've conceived all of his gloom and insecurity
And birthed his future horizons and power without a glimpse of
real dignity
What if you just want someone to call your home away from
home
Someone to suck your neck and call your own
Someone who knows when to curl you in and when to just leave
you alone
Someone who's just like a friend but knows you better than them,
even when y'all are all grown
Who doesn't feel like he's all yours but you share him with the
world
Who doesn't force you to man up or have sons or birth him a girl

Mama.

We are on close but far away islands,
One big,
One small,
We are close enough to hear each other,
But not enough to see at all,
So that the islands are never meant to be equal,
But remain opposite...

I have to quit
I can't live through this
I can't be this
I can't do it
I'm not the same
I'm not for you
You're not for me
But we belong together
As long as we swim and cry
To make it work
Though we already know
How the story goes
One island is blue
One island is red
One island i knew
Could get someone dead
What are we going to do?
Surrounded by nothing but another Blue.

Unless, perhaps, a change is made.
You make it? Or do I?
The doubt rises, and fades.

Island Lady.

I don't think I can live without you.
At least, not unlike this, not for now.
I need you, you are the air I breathe,
The blood that runs in me, the current that sets my brain into a
summer day,
A glimpse of paradise:
A taste of something light but rich and bright,
A smell of something thick and sweet and chewy,
A sight of a new old delight.
I cannot go a day without your voice, your words, your love—
Like an owl needs the stars,
Like a wolf needs the moon,
Like an ocean needs waves,
Like a birthday kid needs a balloon,
I crave your arms, your chest, your belly's embrace around my
arms, my chest, my belly, every night.
You're my birthright.

Birth/Air.

Don't quite know how to do this;
Familiar but unknown–
I may go cold turkey before I cut a turkey with that person,
But it's hard doing this all alone.
I am not a woman of
Giving in or giving up,
But I am not so sure anymore that this was ever love.

Holiday Blues.

What's there to write about,
What can I tell you?
Where should I start?!
All I can do now is fart
Fart out my brain
Fart out my ass
I used to write with so much class
I hate author's block
Subconscious, I just stalk.
I used to be able to write song and fable
Any-day-any-week with ease
I would write as much as I'd please, and more
There was always an expression followed by an expression in store
So,
Like...
What's there to write about?
I won't barely give myself a chance
I know you thought this was a lame writing even at just a glance
I don't really have a life
And I don't really have a story
I just write to refresh myself, keep art alive, and give God All the
Glory
(But I doubt you'd wanna read much really);
Each lesson's got its own theme
And its own meaning--
But nothing you wouldn't assume or haven't before seen.
Irrelevant, irrelevance:
That's what some of the writers do, is bore....
Real messages, real meanings,
That's all that I write for.
That I know for sure.
I hope you give my writing a chance, though-
I hope you let the words in your mind and soul dance, so
You see more of what I see,
Can speak on what I speak,
Feel more of what I feel,
So you know that what I write about, it's real.

One Eleven.

Witch, I already own my own empire,
And I'm going to share,
But... Where's yours
And why you gotta glare?!
Here we go again
I'm always here and back around,
You're always there–
What's it gon' take to get you out the Dummy Chair???

Chairs.

is this person worth the stress
is it goodness-involved, can you confess?
is this really happiness
if it isn't what God would or could bless?
presumed marriage,
presumed carriage,
resumed dating
no real wedding
no real brags--
and def no heard gags;
fallen from fake riches
to colorful rags
may it be
our destiny
or will one
go
somewhere, where
he won't know?

Stress, to Know.

Ya say you like lemonade,
But what about when it gets old
The bitterness grows a stronger bite
The sweetness gone, it don't feel right
The tang and punch is over-soured

You realized that for too long,
You've been empowered
Just by stepping on top of and squashing your girl
Like she's some concubine
You squashed like grapes placed in a tub for wine,
Like the wine you always made her drink
So she wouldn't yell, or speak, just blink
And nod off so you don't have to see or hear what she thinks
About you, about him,
About her faraway friends
Or about what happens once September will commence

In all this chaos,
    are you the only one that makes sense?
      No.
      Besides God,

      Nothing in this home or in this heart
        Is sensible, complete, or my peace.
        Is this alright? Or all right?
        I guess so.

So.

Bob
we just gave you one job
to report before the mob
arose
so no one here would juxtapose
our plot
we gave the fab
up for you to not stop
you know you had the major job–
counting and recording for us
your mission was
most marvelous
yes marvelously made
our vision couldn't fade
into the dust
you knew this was a must
we gave you all our trust
now commander aide's gonna fuss
and she can't blame all of us
so who
has got a single clue
now
that it's all coming down
of what to do
??
?

Lil Minion Mischief.

When I try and breathe and think
What will I put down to ink
I just look down and stare
The page begins to glare,
Back,
As if to say,
What does your entirety lack?
What will it share?
What does it have?
Why is it here,
Right here, and not there,
Hone in,
Let's hone in,
Now, don't compare
Your identity's not in your looks
Your identity's been in the books.

I Try.

Maybe not
But maybe so
Now you know
You'll never know
What an alternative could've been this year:
Maybe you had too much fear
I moved on,
I only left you somewhat
Because something was missing--
Some things are missing
And you barely even see it--
You don't view the source, you see
The sun and its rays, but don't take
In the blue background,
The characters, but not the setting
Of the stage, the branches, but not
Roots, not the seed.
You need insurance...
You need satisfaction...
You need depth..
You need deep love.
Deep light.
Still blind to the source of life
And the spirits of good and bad, and
Yet you wanted to be with me,
But hurt part of me,
Couldn't fathom who I am and what I know.
Now, it's up to you.

One Twelve.

Does He identify with shamin' just cuz
Some things take "too long" or don't go as planned?
Does He identify with self hurt or self harm at all or is it all in
your head??
Even if you do and we do,
He doesn't have that all in His plans.
He has it all in His Hands!

Twelve Thirty.

I peel off my excess skin
'Cause I can't scratch at what is within
I scrape up what is left
Leaving a growing mess.
I like pickin' my head, I like pickin' my scalp
I like pickin' at me, it sets me quite free:
Let go of my doubts!
Ears
Navel
Tears or fears
Queer
I did it as much as I am able
I pick at my forehead,
Oh I get bored dead!
I pick at my back
Ears
Yeah, I know I'm so weird!

Two Sixteen.

blood that's red, or blood that's green, why's that matter
anyways?
don't you know that we still have it in our feet, in our arms, all
inside us
humanity's all over, it's inside my DNA!
can't you see– the *Motherland*–
it runs through *all* our veins,
and yet you throw at them and us and me,
but my royalty remains!

Remains.

I wish I could promise I'd be back there in a sitch,
But I'm a rebellin' hard workin' rave,
Tryin' not to be no one's slave,
I'm a pupil with an itch,
Not so used to being anyone's ol' witch.
I'm just a student under submission,
Tied to a regular angry private school tuition,
I'm just an angel doin' the hustle
Just another devil tryna not pop a joint or pull a muscle...

Eight One.

Some girls and boys
Didn't even know about toys
Till they were treated as such.
That wasn't me,
What a terror to see,
But it hurts me so much.

Is it a mental disease or a game passed down Without cease
Or seizure? Who'll end it?
How can we defend it?

We defend it if we
Allow it to be
The norm any longer.
They're just getting stronger.
Fast like a flutter-by
Hot like your tea
You'll never clean my heart out
Like his showers cleaned me.

Low as a manatee
Stealthy as a fox
You'll never find my secrets
Even under Battlefield rocks.

Dark as the quarry
Iridescent as opals in coal
You'll never reach my bar levels
They're higher than y'all's goals!

Twelve Thirty-1.

Someone
Some kid
Told me they
Hate poetry. That really
Offended me.

Someone.

What the world-a-round was I thinking?
Falling for a silly boy like you,
Thought you were so caring and your eyes Shone like a dream
        Come true–
I feel like I step out of the real world, my real world,
Whenever it's just me and you,
You are sometimes,
        Just sometimes,
                Magical.
                And it's not just the things you do.

Just.

My life is the story of a poem,
and each poem tells a story of my life.
One day,
One hour,
One thought,
One shower,
A poem is for me. It's not for you.
One gaze,
One power,
Thought by thought,
Day by day.
How I see.
What I pray.
It's not for you. It's for we.

It's for me.

Days.

Oh, how I yearn and cry to be able to say,
I've been forgetting & pushing
          away the moments--
                    the memories,
                    the hopes;
                    those smiles,
                    that rub,
                    that nose.
                    The chances taken--
The chances left to cower, envelope
          and die.
You wonder why I don't cry.
You don't know what's behind my eyes.

And sometimes, I don't.
And sometimes, I won't.
Well, sometimes, it varies.
Yes, all times I carry
My weapon, love and sword,
          Holy Spirit; The Holy Word,
          But sometimes, behind these eyes,
                    And this vast mind,
                              I carry
                              A wanting for another
                                        Emptiness,
                              For a leap at one more
                                        Dawn of bliss,
                              For you to have a key,
                              Any key to
                                        This hole--
But it's too late.
Jesus already saved my soul.
And so much more.
Now what's in store?
Sometimes, my flesh & will get
                              Reminded

Of deadly glory,
But it's binded.
I keep tryna ignore,
But I can't hide it,
I'm human and weak,
God I must
Constantly seek.
Or else I'll wreak
& no longer feel meek.

Six Twenty-Nine.

You imagined me as,
You gave me the most eccentrically bright Gerber daisies,
forget-me-nots, tulips, pansies,
You saw me as the most gorgeous lily in a
        valley of nothing but
Stones and dirt and busy prancing deer,
The brightest zinnia in a 500 square foot garden,
The same color, same type, same size,
But I might as well be 50 feet tall and command
        the garden and its hosts.
Or be the shortest and smallest, but tingle and Shine on you like
the Holy Ghost,
You know who I was and
                You loved Me the most,
You didn't care.
You didn't care.
Just me.
In pink

Who I Was.

See, she saw those things different.
She saw the shifting amongst them
        before the truth came out, verbatim.
She saw the laughter before it snuck
        around and exploded anywhere and everywhere.
She also saw lives no one else seemed to.
See, she saw the hopes barely anyone
        around seems to commune with in dreams
        or whatever they're dreaming for.
And those, the folks did see, too.
Together, a few, but many, they saw
The living- thriving, bursting,
Conniving, Preying,
The dead-- sighing, thirsting, new,
        arriving, laying.

They felt music that was never played;
        They stayed informed by words that were never uttered,
They listened to winds which breezed by
        elsewhere,
They read and wrote solutions
        that were never inscribed.
So, often, they'd ask themselves,
        "Why me or why all of <u>us</u>- in this world,
        in this life?"

E.U.N.

Love doesn't have to be logical,
But if you love your friend, you should use common sense.
Love them in a way that won't hurt them.
So, just do what's right.

Friend.

It's been a few months and I still can't get you out of my head
'cause you've stained over my heart.
You're energy's still part of my sight, my sound, my feeling.
It rattles through my hormones, it courses through my organs,
but I don't call it a snake, and it's no disease.
But I gotta, *I gotta* get rid of it.
I can't go on... Something's been missing and I think I know what
it is.
I can't find all my peace and keep thinking
That it usually stems from your soft kiss.

But that's a lie
I can't deny
I can reach the sky
If I move on and try, try, try.
Attempting to rediscover myself, my worth, my faith
It's been a healthy, *zig-zaggy maze*
Every day's a new day
A new adventure,
A new wave;

You're sitting at the shore, picking at the shells,
I've already leaped in and passed many meters,
You're scared of the depth and all the great creatures,

But life's a voyage,
And you can be anchored but still venture where and how you
possibly do, or can--
Standing still, I cannot stand!

Maze.

I write best
When angry
I speak clearest
Once I'm mad
Why is bein' hurt
Gonna make my purest words
Explode--

Or do they implode
What is that
When happy or mellow
Sometimes my words stumble and can truly fail,
But when you've got me angry
I'm able to storm it all
Like fiery hail

Five Eight.

If I never hold you with these charms again, if I never hear,
"I love you" now or then,
I think I'll fucking live
I think I find it life-stakingly awful to place my
    identity/home/significant/patience/general
    beliefs/cares into or onto one individual. Forget that ish!
I'm not perfect, you're not perfect, he's not
    perfect;
So why in the heck would all this adoration
Over me or anyone be necessary,
Or why would I need to eventually have one
    individual to stick with in this life besides
    God?

No Need.

©

Sienna V. Feruzi is an up and coming poet who loves singing, keeping up with fashion and writers on Instagram, and writing tons of poetry and prose. She studied Economics and served as a Bonner Community Service Scholar at Spelman College.